Y0-BBD-415

TALL SHIPS

IN THE ZENITH CITY

Photographs by Dennis O'Hara

Zenith City PRESS

Duluth, Minnesota

Zenith City Press
Duluth, Minnesota
218-310-6541
www.zenithcity.com

Tall ships in the zenith city

Photographs by Dennis O'Hara
(except where noted)

Design and Text by Tony Dierckins
Copy Edit by Scott Pearson
Proofread by Hollis Norman

First Edition, 2013

13 14 15 16 17 • 5 4 3 2 1

Library of Congress Control Number: 2013930729

ISBN: 978-1-887317-39-9

Printed in Brainerd, Minnesota, USA
by Bang Printing

———

Discover more photos by Dennis O'Hara
at www.northernimages.com

———

Front Cover: *Niagara* off Duluth's North Pier Light
Back Cover: *Zeeto, Niagara,* and *Pride of
Baltimore II* off Duluth's South Pier Light
Title Page: ship's bell from the *Niagara*
Left: mast and rigging, *HMS Bounty*
Opposite: figurehead, *HMS Bounty*
Contents Page: rigging, *Niagara*

Zenith City Press & Northern Images would like to thank:

Dexter Donham; C. Pat Labadie; Davis Helberg;
Laura Jacobs & the Lake Superior Maritime Collection;
Gene Shaw, Terry Mattson, and VisitDuluth;
Criag Samborski and Draw Events.

Ship biographies and statistical information adapted from the following sources:

Sail Tall Ships, 19th Edition
(Tall Ships America, Newport, RI, 2011)

tallshipbounty.org; superiorodyssey.com;
discoveryworld.org; barkeuropa.com;
privateerlynx.com; maritimeheritagealliance.org;
eriemaritimemuseum.org; fullriggeren-sorlandet.no;
pride2.org; sailtraining.de; sailingshipadventures.com;
baysailbaycity.org, peacemakermarine.com;
tallshipadventuresofchicago.com

Research for "Tall Ships on Lake Superior":

Pride of the Inland Seas by Bill Beck and C. Patrick
Labadie (Afton Historical Society Press, 2004).

"History and Development of Great Lakes Water Craft,"
from *Minnesota's Lake Superior Shipwrecks A.D.
1650-1945* by C. Patrick Labadie, Brina J. Agranat
and Scott Anfinson (www.mnhs.org).

Guest Photographs
Peacemaker (p. 55) Yat12t/CC-BY-SA
Sørlandet (p. 56) West Island College International
Hindu (p. 57) sailschoonerhindu.com
Halie & Matthew (p. 58) easternmaineimages.com

A Note on 2013 Vessels
The ships included herein as participants of
Tall Ships Duluth 2013 were confirmed as
this book went to press; there may have been
additions or cancellations since that time.

Contents

Duluth in 1883

Tall Ships on Lake Superior

Tall ships first sailed the Great Lakes in 1679, when Robert Sieur de La Salle built a seventy-foot galliot above Niagara Falls and named it the *Griffon*. The *Griffon* and other early Great Lakes' vessels—brigs, schooners, and sloops—were modeled after traditional European designs.

Until Louis Denis Monsieur de LaRonde arrived at Saulte St. Marie nearly midway through the eighteenth century, shipping traffic on Lake Superior was limited to canoes and barge-like batteaux, used by both native tribes and French voyageurs and missionaries. In 1734 de LaRonde established a ship building community along the St. Mary's River at Point Aux Pins, six miles west of Saulte Ste. Marie in what was then known as New France (today it is both Michigan and Ontario). That year he built a twenty-five-ton vessel rigged with two sails, hoping to cash in on the copper mines he established at Ontonogan, Michigan, on the Upper Peninsula. But Michigan's copper mines wouldn't be functioning at a high enough capacity for another hundred years.

In 1771, Alexander Henry and Alexander Baxter built another forty-ton ship at Point Aux Pins to once again exploit copper mining, but they were also too early for Michigan's copper mining industry. Beginning in 1786 the Northwest Company, a fur trapping firm, built several forty- to sixty-ton schooners at Point Aux Pins named the *Athabaska*, the *Otter*, the *Perseverance*, the *Fur Trader*, the *Invincible*, and the *Discovery*. Two other North West ships, the *Mink* and the *Recovery*, were built at Fort William, Ontario. Smaller sailing craft known as Mackinaw boats were also used during this period. Still, until the 1820s fewer than five sailing vessels were in service on Lake Superior at any one time.

Following the War of 1812, during which they were used heavily, schooners became the Great Lakes vessels of choice. Most merchant ships built after the war and prior to 1830 were two-masted schooners. About seventy feet in length, each carried approximately 150 tons of cargo and required a crew of three or four men. Beginning in the 1830s brigantines became popular, remaining so until about 1850. But they proved difficult to maneuver and required a crew twice the size of a schooner's, so they were too expensive to operate at a profit.

The *Algonquin* was portaged along the St. Mary's River at Saulte Ste. Marie onto Lake Superior in 1840. (Image: Lake Superior Maritime Collection.)

Islands). The Hudson's Bay Company also tried its hand at commercial fishing, launching the *Whitefish* in 1836 and later portaging the *Mary Elisabeth* around the falls of the St. Mary's River to Lake Superior. The catch was impressive, but the market for fresh fish was small—and then disappeared after the 1837 financial panic. The fur company gave up on fishing before 1840. The

As the fur trade declined, some of these vessels were dismantled or moved to one of the lower lakes. John Jacob Astor's American Fur Company tried its hand at fishing Lake Superior, building the 111-ton schooner *John Jacob Astor* at Point Aux Pins in 1835 to transport fish and supplies. The firm added two more vessels over the next few years, the *Madeline* and the *William Brewster* (the latter was constructed at La Pointe on Madeline Island in the Apostle *Astor*, considered the first American commercial vessel to sail Lake Superior, sank September 21, 1844, at the Superior Fort Williams dock in Copper Harbor, Michigan.

Despite this, some historians regard the *Algonquin* as "the first vessel to trade at the head of the lakes." The schooner was built in 1839 and in 1840 it was portaged around the rapids of the St. Mary River, which connects Lake Superior and Lake Michigan, using "rollers" (likely logs). Some claim that until the locks at Saulte Ste. Marie opened in 1855, the *Algonquin* enjoyed monopolizing commercial traffic on Lake Superior, but according to the city of Saulte Ste. Marie, the vessels built at Point Aux Pins and at least nine other schooners were on Lake Superior in 1846. (The *Algonquin* was abandoned in 1865 at Superior, Wisconsin.)

By the time the 1854 Treaty of La Pointe opened Lake Superior's North Shore to American settlement and the locks at Saulte St. Marie opened the following year, the shipping world was already transforming from sail to steam. The financial Panic of 1857 and the onset of the Civil War a few years later delayed most settlement—and therefore ship traffic—in the region until the mid 1860s.

A boom in shipbuilding followed the Civil War, and during this time shipwrights made three-masted vessels 150 to 170 feet in length, nearly double the size of their predecessors, indicating a shift in shipping: as the country became crisscrossed with more and more railroads, the lakes would become the highway for

salt, grain, coal, and lumber. The new vessels were designed as freighters to carry these and other bulk goods.

In March 1870 Duluth first became a city. That same year the Lake Superior & Mississippi Railroad finished its connection from Duluth to St. Paul and built a warehouse, grain elevator, dock, and breakwater at the very corner of Lake Superior, along the shore between Third and Fourth Avenues West.

A year earlier shipbuilding began in Duluth. Lewis Merritt, his son Alfred, and Edmund Ely built the *Chaska*, a seventy-two-foot-long schooner and the largest ship in Duluth at the time. Unfortunately, the vessel was battered to pieces a year later off the shore of Michigan's Upper Peninsula.

The schooner was already on its way out. Throughout the 1880s, bulk freighters powered by both sail and steam and steam-powered vessels such as the *Meteor* (shown in the postcard, left)

A lithographic postcard manufactured in 1908 using a negative of a photograph taken June 3, 1871, when Duluth was less than two years old. Elevator A is shown at right, while two schooners wait to be loaded. At left is the steamer *Meteor*. (Image: Zenith City Press.)

took passengers and goods to and from Duluth. In the 1870s Napoleon Grignon opened his first shipyard along Minnesota Point at Buchanan Street in what is today the Canal Park Business District, later moving his operation to the foot of Eleventh Avenue West. By 1880 his focus had already moved away from wooden sailing vessels as he incorporated the Marine Iron and Shipbuilding Company and turned his attention to metal-clad, steam-powered vessels.

Built in 1873, the *D. M. Wilson* represented the first generation of bulk-freighters on Lake Superior, propelled by sail and steam. (Image: C. Patrick Labidie.)

The construction of fully-rigged sailing vessels on the Great Lakes declined heavily in the 1880s, and 1889 saw the launching of the last large schooner on the lakes. Any sail-powered craft built for the Great Lakes from that point had short masts and were used as tow-barges; few of these measured up to three hundred feet. A handful of schooners continued into the twentieth century, but were rarely profitable. Schooners *Our Son* and *Lyman M. Davis*, the last on Lake Superior, ceased operating in the 1930s.

Since that time, sailed vessels that have visited the Zenith City (or have called the port home) have for the most part been small pleasure craft or reconstructions of historic vessels. In fact, a few years before the *Our Son* and the *Lyman M. Davis* went out of service, Duluth celebrated the arrival of the first reconstruction of a historic sailing vessel to reach Duluth: the *Leif Erikson*.

She was not a very tall ship. The *Erikson* was built in Norway in 1926 for Captain Gerhard Folgero. According to historian Pat Labadie, the *Leif Erikson* was a forty-two-foot wooden "femboring" craft "patterned after the traditional Norwegian working craft that served coastal shippers and fisherfolk for centuries [and was] used by medieval Norse adventurers and explorers." So the *Leif Erikson* was not a precise replica of a Viking craft but a representation of the same class and style of boat likely used by Leif Erikson himself. The vessel itself was not nearly as remarkable as the journey she took.

Captain Folgero and his crew outfitted the *Erikson* with carved head and tail pieces and wooden shields bearing Viking devices, then sailed the dressed-up fishing boat from Bergen, Norway, to the coast of Labrador and beyond, supposedly following much of Leif Erikson's original 1002 route.

It wasn't easy. They faced hurricane-like winds, icebergs, and weeks of fog. But they made it to Labrador and on to Boston, covering 6,700 miles in fifty days. From Boston they sailed on to Duluth to take part in a national convention of Norwegian emigrants. By the time they arrived in the Zenith City, the *Erikson* and her crew had covered roughly 10,000 miles. That they accomplished this in a forty-two-foot boat outfitted with only oars and a square sail is nothing short of remarkable.

That's when congressman William Carss suggested Duluthians raise funds to purchase the ship and move it to Lakeshore Park, then rename the park in the boat's honor. But it was Bert Enger and Emil Olson, West End furniture dealers and Norwegian immigrants, who purchased the boat and gave it to Duluth for all to enjoy, and indeed Lakeshore Park was rechristened Leif Erikson Park. The ship remains in the park, but is in need of renovation—and a structure to house it.

Other replica sailing vessels have since visited the Zenith City, including the *Christian Radich* in 1976, *T. S. Merkur* in 1985, *Victory Chimes* in 1986, *Pride of Baltimore II* in 1989, the *HMS Rose* in 1994, and the

The *Leif Erikson* in the Duluth Ship Canal, 1927. (Photograph: Tom Kasper.)

Three tall ships are escorted to port by dozens of pleasure craft while thousands of sightseers gather on the North Pier of the Duluth Ship Canal during the 2008 Tall Ships Festival. (Image: Dennis O'Hara)

U.S. Brig *Niagara* in 2002. The popularity of these visits convinced VisitDuluth to organize the Tall Ships Duluth festival. The 2008 event drew thousands of tourists to Duluth—a great deal more than was expected. The *Denis Sullivan* visited Duluth alone in 2009, and in 2010 the Tall Ships Festival was back—and bigger than ever, with eight ships participating. Three more tall ships—*Niagra, Lynx,* and *Pride of Baltimore II*—visited in 2011.

Tall Ships Duluth 2013 features five vessels that have visited Duluth on past visits as well as four ships that have never passed through the Duluth Ship Canal. The *Niagara, Pride of Baltimore II, Denis Sullivan, Lynx,* and *Coaster II* all return to the Zenith City. Vessels new to Duluth include the *Sørlandet,* the *Peacemaker,* the *Halie & Matthew,* and the *Hindu*

Tall Ships Duluth is lucky to have the *Niagara* returning in 2013. The vessel is in great demand as the year marks the 100th anniversary of the War of 1812's Battle of Lake Erie, during which the *Niagara* was commandeered by Commodore Oliver Hazard Perry after the cannon on his ship, the *Lawrence,* were disabled. The *Niagara* then became the flagship of Perry's Great Lakes fleet.

— Tony Dierckins

Tall Ships in the Zenith City

(2008–2011)

The *Pride of Baltimore II* passing under the Aerial Lift Bridge, 2008.

The *Pride of Baltimore II* (left) and *Niagara* engage in a demonstration battle with the Duluth hillside as a backdrop, 2011.

The *Denis Sullivan* (left) and *Europa* docked in Duluth, 2010.

The *Roseway* anchored on Lake Superior at dawn, 2010.

The *Bounty* navigating the Duluth Ship Canal, 2010.

Bell, cannon, and rigging of the *Bounty*, 2010.

The *Coaster II* in the Duluth Ship Canal, 2010.

The *Lynx (left)* and *Pride of Baltimore II* behind the Duluth Ship Canal's Rear Range Light, 2011.

The *Roald Amundson* passing the South Pier Light, 2010.

The *Niagara* on Lake Superior off the Duluth Ship Canal's South Pier Light, 2011.

Wheel, cannon, and mast of the *Pride of Baltimore II*, 2011.

Pride of Baltimore II passing under the Aerial Lift Bridge, 2011.

Vessels docked behind the Duluth Entertainment & Convention Center on a foggy day, 2010.

The *Denis Sullivan* anchored in the Duluth Harbor, 2010.

The *Pride of Baltimore II* (left) docked in 2008; the *Bounty* docked in 2010.

The *Niagara (left)* and *Pride of Baltimore II* on Lake Superior, 2010.

The *Europa* navigating the Duluth Ship Canal, 2010.

Rigging, figurehead, and mast of the *Europa*, 2010.

The *Niagara* docked in Duluth, 2010.

The *Niagara* photographed from the Aerial Lift Bridge, 2011.

The *Pride of Baltimore II* near the Duluth Ship Canal's South Pier Light, 2011.

The *Bounty* (left) on Lake Superior, 2010; the *Pride of Baltimore* and the *Niagara* (at right), docked in Duluth, 2008.

Mast and rigging of the *Niagara*, 2008.

Ship's bell of the *Niagara (left)*; the *Niagara* passing the North Pier Light, 2010.

The *Lynx* passing near the Duluth Ship Canal's North Pier Light, 2011.

Walking the rigging of the *Lynx*, 2011.

The *Roseway* passing under the Aerial Lift Bridge, 2010.

The *Pride of Baltimore* (left) and *Lynx* on Lake Superior, 2011.

Anchor and bell of the *Lynx*, 2011.

The *Lynx* (right) with the retired Coast Guard cutter *Sundew* in the Duluth Harbor, 2011.

Vessels docked behind the Duluth Entertainment and Convention Center, 2011.

The *Roseway*, framed by the Aerial Lift Bridge, photographed from the deck of the *Pride of Baltimore II*, 2010.

The *Roseway* anchored in the Duluth Harbor, 2010.

Anchor, ship's wheel, and bell from of *Roseway*, 2010.

The *Niagara* navigating the Duluth Ship Canal with the Duluth hillside—including the "antenna farm"—in the background, 2010.

MAY HIS KIND, GE
SMILING SPIRIT FO
AND BRING TO SA
WHO SAIL ON
HER PRO

PRIDE OF TH

SHIP
BIOGRAPHIES

HMS BOUNTY

Perhaps the most well-known tall ship, the *Bounty* was built in 1961, commissioned by MGM Studios for the film *Mutiny on the Bounty* starring Marlon Brando—and then went on to appear in *Yellow Beard* (1983), *Pirates* (1986), *Treasure Island* (1990), *Spongebob SquarePants the Movie* (2004), and two of the *Pirates of the Caribbean* movies.

When she wasn't being filmed, the *Bounty* served as a training vessel, her full-time, paid eighteen-person crew working with trainees and passengers. She offered private and group day sails and was open for dock-side tours, educational programs, and private functions. Her mission focused strongly on youth education. Sadly, in 2012 the *Bounty* sank off the coast of North Carolina trying to avoid Hurricane Sandy. Long-time captain Robin Wallbridge and deckhand Claudene Christian went down with their ship.

LYNX

The modern *Lynx* is a reproduction based on the original *Lynx*, a Baltimore Clipper commissioned at the beginning of the War of 1812 which served as a blockade runner.

Today's *Lynx* has been described as a living museum. She is fitted with period ordnance, including four cannonades and two swivel guns, and flies the colors of the 1812 era. Even the crew wears period uniforms and "operate the ship in keeping with the maritime traditions of early nineteenth-century America."

When not touring, the *Lynx* works as a sail training vessel, offering classes on historical, environmental, and ecological issues. Each summer the Lynx offers a chance to sail to Hawaii and back on what her crew calls "cruises of opportunity."

Dedicated to "all those who cherish the blessings of America," the *Lynx* operates under the credo "be excellent to each other and to your ship."

Vessel: *Lynx*
Rig: Square Topsail Schooner
Era: Late 18th to early 19th Century
Gross Tonnage: 94
Sparred Length: 122' (37m)
Length on Deck: 76' (23m)
Rig Height: 94' (29m)
Beam: 23' (7m)
Draft: 9' (2.7m)
Launched: July 28, 2001
Builder: Rockport Marine, Rockport, Maine
Owner: Lynx Educational Foundation
Home Port: Newport Beach, CA
Duluth Visits: 2011

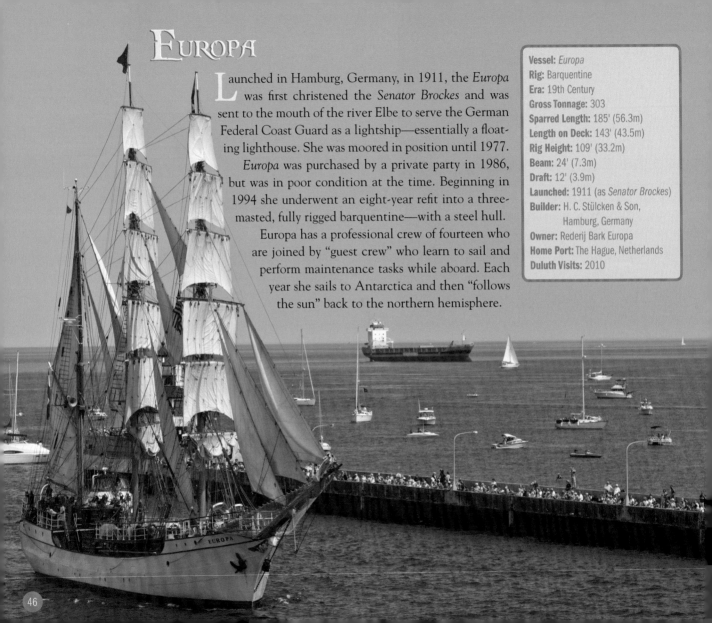

EUROPA

Launched in Hamburg, Germany, in 1911, the *Europa* was first christened the *Senator Brockes* and was sent to the mouth of the river Elbe to serve the German Federal Coast Guard as a lightship—essentially a floating lighthouse. She was moored in position until 1977.

Europa was purchased by a private party in 1986, but was in poor condition at the time. Beginning in 1994 she underwent an eight-year refit into a three-masted, fully rigged barquentine—with a steel hull.

Europa has a professional crew of fourteen who are joined by "guest crew" who learn to sail and perform maintenance tasks while aboard. Each year she sails to Antarctica and then "follows the sun" back to the northern hemisphere.

Vessel: *Europa*
Rig: Barquentine
Era: 19th Century
Gross Tonnage: 303
Sparred Length: 185' (56.3m)
Length on Deck: 143' (43.5m)
Rig Height: 109' (33.2m)
Beam: 24' (7.3m)
Draft: 12' (3.9m)
Launched: 1911 (as *Senator Brockes*)
Builder: H. C. Stülcken & Son, Hamburg, Germany
Owner: Rederij Bark Europa
Home Port: The Hague, Netherlands
Duluth Visits: 2010

Niagara

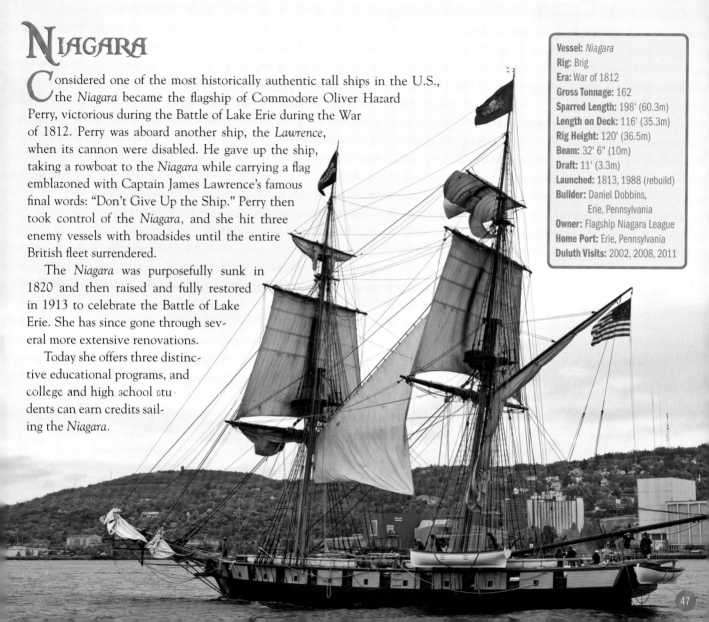

Considered one of the most historically authentic tall ships in the U.S., the *Niagara* became the flagship of Commodore Oliver Hazard Perry, victorious during the Battle of Lake Erie during the War of 1812. Perry was aboard another ship, the *Lawrence*, when its cannon were disabled. He gave up the ship, taking a rowboat to the *Niagara* while carrying a flag emblazoned with Captain James Lawrence's famous final words: "Don't Give Up the Ship." Perry then took control of the *Niagara*, and she hit three enemy vessels with broadsides until the entire British fleet surrendered.

The *Niagara* was purposefully sunk in 1820 and then raised and fully restored in 1913 to celebrate the Battle of Lake Erie. She has since gone through several more extensive renovations.

Today she offers three distinctive educational programs, and college and high school students can earn credits sailing the *Niagara*.

Vessel: *Niagara*
Rig: Brig
Era: War of 1812
Gross Tonnage: 162
Sparred Length: 198' (60.3m)
Length on Deck: 116' (35.3m)
Rig Height: 120' (36.5m)
Beam: 32' 6" (10m)
Draft: 11' (3.3m)
Launched: 1813, 1988 (rebuild)
Builder: Daniel Dobbins, Erie, Pennsylvania
Owner: Flagship Niagara League
Home Port: Erie, Pennsylvania
Duluth Visits: 2002, 2008, 2011

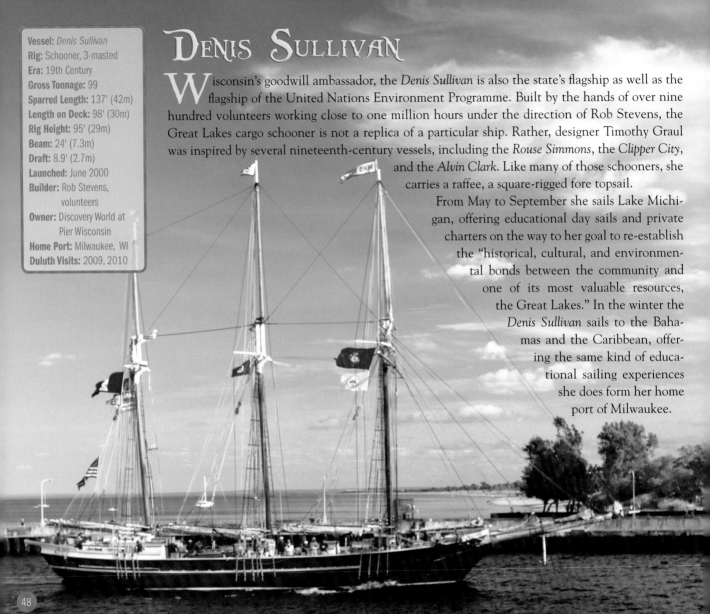

Denis Sullivan

Vessel: *Denis Sullivan*
Rig: Schooner, 3-masted
Era: 19th Century
Gross Tonnage: 99
Sparred Length: 137' (42m)
Length on Deck: 98' (30m)
Rig Height: 95' (29m)
Beam: 24' (7.3m)
Draft: 8.9' (2.7m)
Launched: June 2000
Builder: Rob Stevens,
    volunteers
Owner: Discovery World at
    Pier Wisconsin
Home Port: Milwaukee, WI
Duluth Visits: 2009, 2010

Wisconsin's goodwill ambassador, the *Denis Sullivan* is also the state's flagship as well as the flagship of the United Nations Environment Programme. Built by the hands of over nine hundred volunteers working close to one million hours under the direction of Rob Stevens, the Great Lakes cargo schooner is not a replica of a particular ship. Rather, designer Timothy Graul was inspired by several nineteenth-century vessels, including the *Rouse Simmons*, the *Clipper City*, and the *Alvin Clark*. Like many of those schooners, she carries a raffee, a square-rigged fore topsail.

From May to September she sails Lake Michigan, offering educational day sails and private charters on the way to her goal to re-establish the "historical, cultural, and environmental bonds between the community and one of its most valuable resources, the Great Lakes." In the winter the *Denis Sullivan* sails to the Bahamas and the Caribbean, offering the same kind of educational sailing experiences she does form her home port of Milwaukee.

ROALD AMUNDSEN

Named for Norwegian polar explorer Roald Engelbregt Gravning Amundsen (1872–1928), this brig first took to the water to serve the East German military as a deep-sea fishing lugger. After the fall of the Berlin Wall rendered her unnecessary, she was abandoned in Wolgast, Germany. In 1992 she was discovered by sail enthusiasts, stripped to the hull, and converted into a two-masted brig. She now serves as a sail-training vessel.

Roald Amundsen led the first crossing of the Northwest Passage, the first successful expedition to the South Pole, and was the first expedition leader to reach the North Pole.

Vessel: *Roald Amundsen*
Rig: Brig
Era: 19th Century
Gross Tonnage: 284
Length Over All: 130' (50.2m)
Length on Deck: 125' (40.8m)
Rig Height: 105' (34m)
Beam: 24' (7.2m)
Draft: 14' (4.2m)
Launched: 1952, converted 1992
Builder: East Germany
Owner: LLaS e.V.
Home Port: Eckernford, Germany
Duluth Visits: 2010

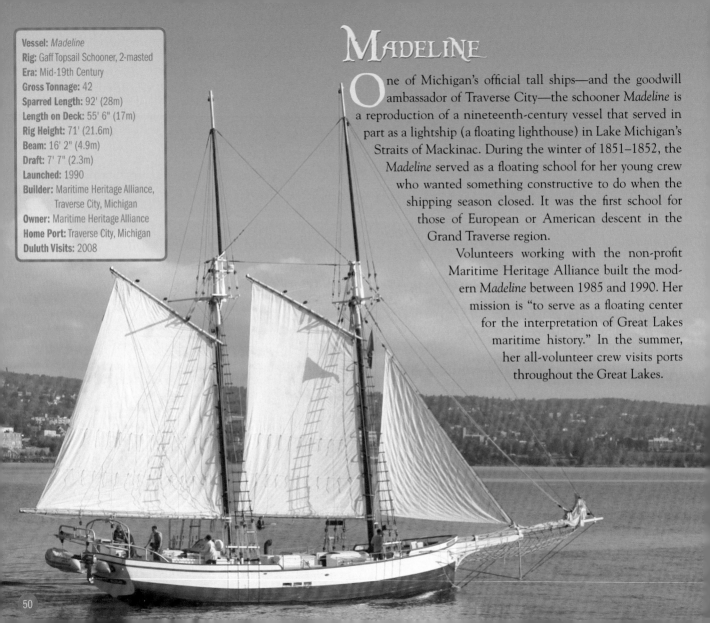

MADELINE

One of Michigan's official tall ships—and the goodwill ambassador of Traverse City—the schooner *Madeline* is a reproduction of a nineteenth-century vessel that served in part as a lightship (a floating lighthouse) in Lake Michigan's Straits of Mackinac. During the winter of 1851–1852, the *Madeline* served as a floating school for her young crew who wanted something constructive to do when the shipping season closed. It was the first school for those of European or American descent in the Grand Traverse region.

Volunteers working with the non-profit Maritime Heritage Alliance built the modern *Madeline* between 1985 and 1990. Her mission is "to serve as a floating center for the interpretation of Great Lakes maritime history." In the summer, her all-volunteer crew visits ports throughout the Great Lakes.

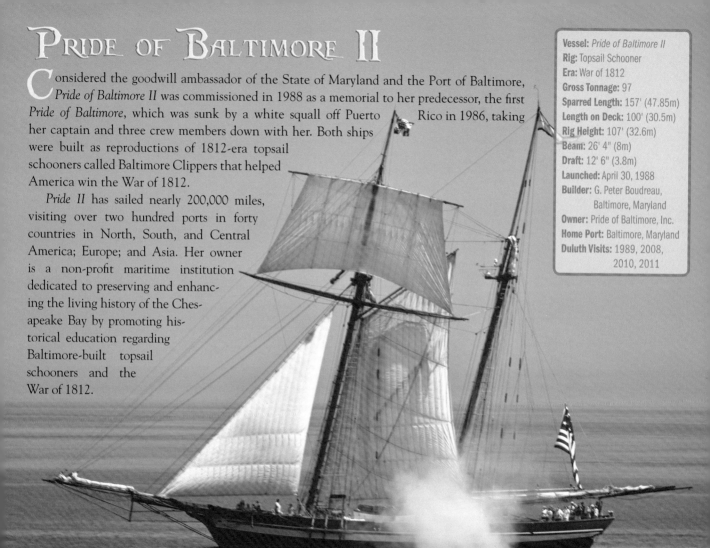

PRIDE OF BALTIMORE II

Considered the goodwill ambassador of the State of Maryland and the Port of Baltimore, *Pride of Baltimore II* was commissioned in 1988 as a memorial to her predecessor, the first *Pride of Baltimore*, which was sunk by a white squall off Puerto Rico in 1986, taking her captain and three crew members down with her. Both ships were built as reproductions of 1812-era topsail schooners called Baltimore Clippers that helped America win the War of 1812.

Pride II has sailed nearly 200,000 miles, visiting over two hundred ports in forty countries in North, South, and Central America; Europe; and Asia. Her owner is a non-profit maritime institution dedicated to preserving and enhancing the living history of the Chesapeake Bay by promoting historical education regarding Baltimore-built topsail schooners and the War of 1812.

Vessel: *Pride of Baltimore II*
Rig: Topsail Schooner
Era: War of 1812
Gross Tonnage: 97
Sparred Length: 157' (47.85m)
Length on Deck: 100' (30.5m)
Rig Height: 107' (32.6m)
Beam: 26' 4" (8m)
Draft: 12' 6" (3.8m)
Launched: April 30, 1988
Builder: G. Peter Boudreau, Baltimore, Maryland
Owner: Pride of Baltimore, Inc.
Home Port: Baltimore, Maryland
Duluth Visits: 1989, 2008, 2010, 2011

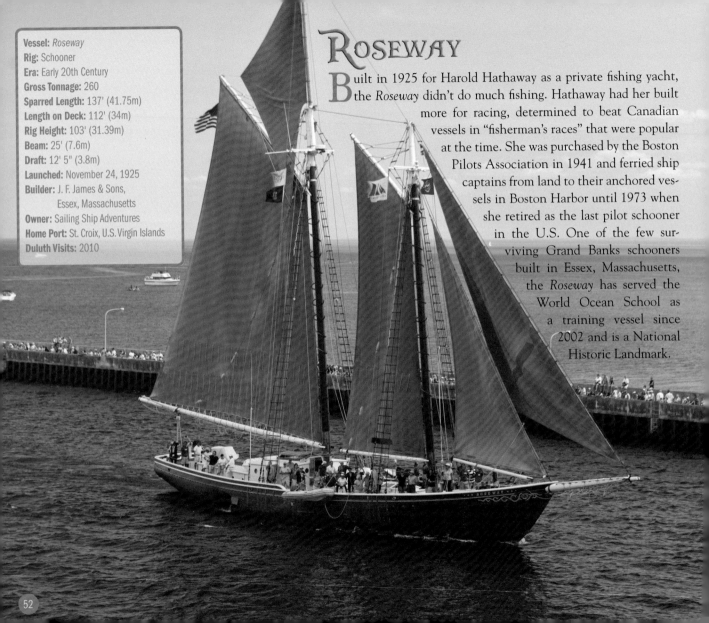

Vessel: *Roseway*
Rig: Schooner
Era: Early 20th Century
Gross Tonnage: 260
Sparred Length: 137' (41.75m)
Length on Deck: 112' (34m)
Rig Height: 103' (31.39m)
Beam: 25' (7.6m)
Draft: 12' 5" (3.8m)
Launched: November 24, 1925
Builder: J. F. James & Sons,
    Essex, Massachusetts
Owner: Sailing Ship Adventures
Home Port: St. Croix, U.S. Virgin Islands
Duluth Visits: 2010

ROSEWAY

Built in 1925 for Harold Hathaway as a private fishing yacht, the *Roseway* didn't do much fishing. Hathaway had her built more for racing, determined to beat Canadian vessels in "fisherman's races" that were popular at the time. She was purchased by the Boston Pilots Association in 1941 and ferried ship captains from land to their anchored vessels in Boston Harbor until 1973 when she retired as the last pilot schooner in the U.S. One of the few surviving Grand Banks schooners built in Essex, Massachusetts, the *Roseway* has served the World Ocean School as a training vessel since 2002 and is a National Historic Landmark.

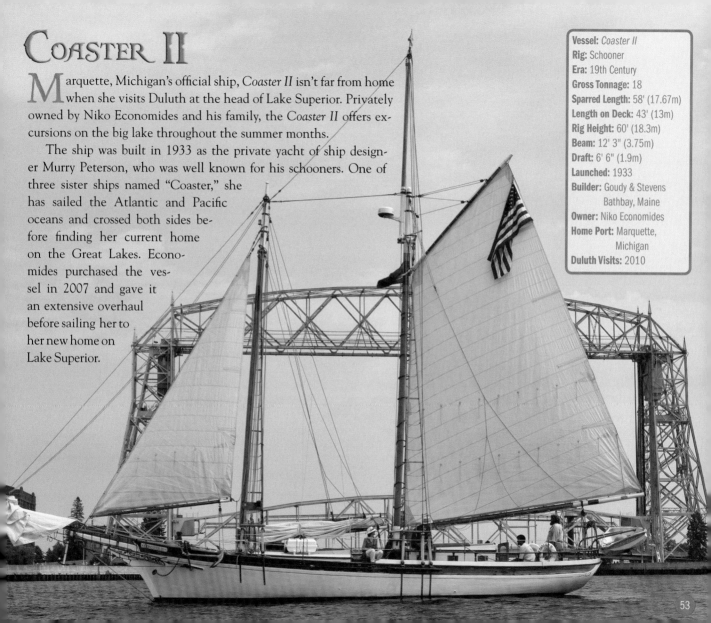

COASTER II

Marquette, Michigan's official ship, *Coaster II* isn't far from home when she visits Duluth at the head of Lake Superior. Privately owned by Niko Economides and his family, the *Coaster II* offers excursions on the big lake throughout the summer months.

The ship was built in 1933 as the private yacht of ship designer Murry Peterson, who was well known for his schooners. One of three sister ships named "Coaster," she has sailed the Atlantic and Pacific oceans and crossed both sides before finding her current home on the Great Lakes. Economides purchased the vessel in 2007 and gave it an extensive overhaul before sailing her to her new home on Lake Superior.

Vessel: *Coaster II*
Rig: Schooner
Era: 19th Century
Gross Tonnage: 18
Sparred Length: 58' (17.67m)
Length on Deck: 43' (13m)
Rig Height: 60' (18.3m)
Beam: 12' 3" (3.75m)
Draft: 6' 6" (1.9m)
Launched: 1933
Builder: Goudy & Stevens
Bathbay, Maine
Owner: Niko Economides
Home Port: Marquette,
Michigan
Duluth Visits: 2010

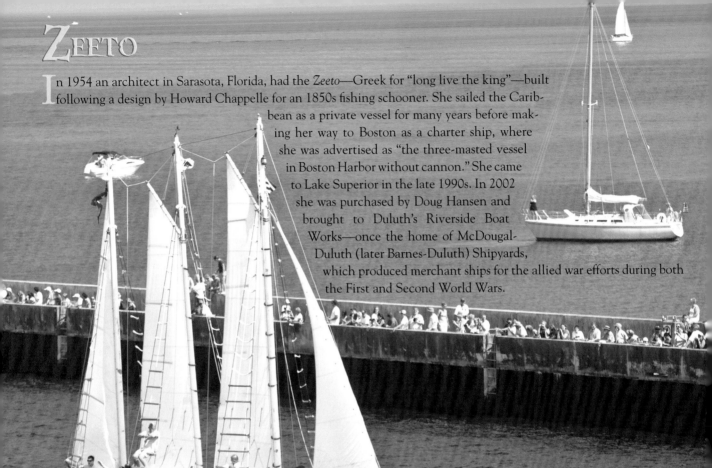

ZEETO

In 1954 an architect in Sarasota, Florida, had the *Zeeto*—Greek for "long live the king"—built following a design by Howard Chappelle for an 1850s fishing schooner. She sailed the Caribbean as a private vessel for many years before making her way to Boston as a charter ship, where she was advertised as "the three-masted vessel in Boston Harbor without cannon." She came to Lake Superior in the late 1990s. In 2002 she was purchased by Doug Hansen and brought to Duluth's Riverside Boat Works—once the home of McDougal-Duluth (later Barnes-Duluth) Shipyards, which produced merchant ships for the allied war efforts during both the First and Second World Wars.

Vessel: *Zeeto*
Rig: Schooner, 2-masted
Era: 1850s
Gross Tonnage: 21' (6.4m)
Sparred Length: 54' (16.45m)
Length on Deck: 45' (13.7m)
Rig Height: 42' (12.8m)

Beam: 14' 6" (4.4m)
Draft: 6' 11" (2m)
Launched: 1954
Builder: Sarasota, Florida
Owner: Doug Hansen
Home Port: Bayfield, Wisconsin
Duluth Visits: 2010, 2013

PEACEMAKER

A family of Italian boat builders constructed this vessel on a riverbank in southern Brazil at the behest of Brazilian industrialist Frank Walker in 1989 using traditional methods and tropical hardwoods. Walker motored the ship, first christened *Avany*, to Savannah, Georgia, intending to rig it and operate it as a charter vessel. Walker never finished the job. In 2000 Twelve Tribes, a religious group with more than fifty communities in North and South America, Europe, and Australia—purchased the *Avany* and spent seven years refitting her as a barquentine. The vessel was rechristened the *Peacemaker* when she was relaunched in 2007.

Twelve Tribes uses the *Peacemaker* in part to sail between its communities throughout the world, offering apprenticeship opportunities and cross-cultural experiences to its youth.

Vessel: *Peacemaker*
Rig: Barquentine
Era: 19th Century
Gross Tonnage: 400
Sparred Length: 150' (45.7m)
Length on Deck: 124' (37.8m)
Rig Height: 123' (37.5m)
Beam: 10' (3m)
Draft: 14' (4.2m)
Launched: 1989, 2007
Builder: Maccarini Shipyards Navegantes, SC, Brazil
Owner: Peacemaker Marine
Home Port: Savannah, GA
Duluth Visits: 2013

SØRLANDET

Launched in 1927 as a national merchant marine training ship, the *Sørlandet* is the oldest full-rigged ship in operation today (older ships exist, but they are not square-rigged, three-masted vessels). During her maiden voyage to Oslo in 1927, the *Sørlandet* was inspected by King Haakon VII of Norway and his son, Crown Prince Olav. Olav would visit Duluth in 1939 to dedicate Enger Tower, built to commemorate Duluth parks benefactor Bert Enger, a Norwegian immigrant. In 1933 she represented Norway at Chicago's Century of Progress Exposition.

During the summer the *Sørlandet* offers paying trainees from fifteen to seventy years old the chance to learn to crew on a traditional sailing ship. In the fall and winter she works with West Island College International's Class Afloat program in Montreal, which lost its vessel, the *Concordia*, in 2010.

Vessel: *Sørlandet*
Rig: Fully Rigged Ship
Era: 19th Century
Gross Tonnage: 499
Sparred Length: 210' 4" (64.15m)
Length on Deck: 186' (56.69m)
Rig Height: 112' (34.2m)
Beam: 29' (8.87m)
Draft: 14' 7" (4.46m)
Launched: 1927
Builder: Høivolds Mek. Verksted, Kristiansand, Norway
Owner: The Ship Sørlandet Foundation
Home Port: Kristiansand, Norway
Duluth Visits: 2013

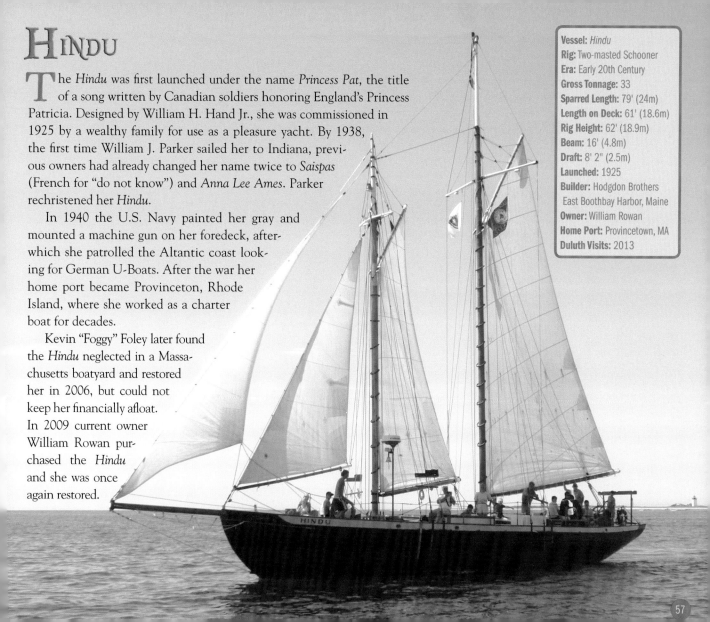

HINDU

The *Hindu* was first launched under the name *Princess Pat*, the title of a song written by Canadian soldiers honoring England's Princess Patricia. Designed by William H. Hand Jr., she was commissioned in 1925 by a wealthy family for use as a pleasure yacht. By 1938, the first time William J. Parker sailed her to Indiana, previous owners had already changed her name twice to *Saispas* (French for "do not know") and *Anna Lee Ames*. Parker rechristened her *Hindu*.

In 1940 the U.S. Navy painted her gray and mounted a machine gun on her foredeck, after-which she patrolled the Altantic coast looking for German U-Boats. After the war her home port became Provinceton, Rhode Island, where she worked as a charter boat for decades.

Kevin "Foggy" Foley later found the *Hindu* neglected in a Massachusetts boatyard and restored her in 2006, but could not keep her financially afloat. In 2009 current owner William Rowan purchased the *Hindu* and she was once again restored.

Vessel: *Hindu*
Rig: Two-masted Schooner
Era: Early 20th Century
Gross Tonnage: 33
Sparred Length: 79' (24m)
Length on Deck: 61' (18.6m)
Rig Height: 62' (18.9m)
Beam: 16' (4.8m)
Draft: 8' 2" (2.5m)
Launched: 1925
Builder: Hodgdon Brothers
 East Boothbay Harbor, Maine
Owner: William Rowan
Home Port: Provincetown, MA
Duluth Visits: 2013

Halie & Matthew

Vessel: *Halie & Matthew*
Rig: Schooner
Era: 19th Century
Gross Tonnage: 102
Sparred Length: 118' (35.9m)
Length on Deck: 90' 2" (27.5m)
Rig Height: 85' (25.9m)
Beam: 24' 6" (7.46m)
Draft: 12' (3.65m)
Launched: 2005
Builder: Captain Butch Harris
Owner: Marine Windjammers
Home Port: Eastport, ME
Duluth Visits: 2013

Captain Butch Harris took just over six years to construct this schooner, which follows a traditional design but was built with a solid fiberglass hull. After the *Halie & Matthew* was launched in 2005, Captain Harris operated her as a charter whale-watching vessel, taking passengers from Maine to Nova Scotia. A few years later the ship's home port was relocated to Key West, Florida, where she helped Boy Scouts earn badges sailing from the Keys to Dry Tortugas National Park. The park, a series of small islands located roughly seventy miles west of Key West, is home to Fort Jefferson, which was built in 1847 as an advance post to protect the Gulf Coast from naval attack. In 2010 the *Halie & Matthew* participated in relief efforts for survivors of the earthquake in Haiti, carrying over 45,000 pounds of supplies. In July 2013 the *Halie & Matthew* made her way to Chicago to sail under the direction of Lakeshore Sail Charters and alongside the *Windy*, a traditional 148-foot four-masted topsail schooner.

Featured vessels that have visited Duluth:

Previous tall ship visits to Duluth:

Christian Radich, 1976

T. S. Merkur, 1985

Victory Chimes, 1986

HMS Rose, 1994

Right: *HMS Bounty*

Tall Ships in the Zenith City is a collaborative effort from:

Tall Ships Duluth 2013 festival organizer VisitDuluth—the Zenith City's convention and visitors' bureau—is dedicated to promoting the area as one of America's great vacation and meeting destinations while providing comprehensive, unbiased information to all travelers. Visit VisitDuluth at:

www.VisitDuluth.com

Photographer Dennis O'Hara's work can be found at Northern Images Photography, where you can purchase prints of the photos in this book—and many others. See more at:

www.northernimages.com

Northern Images also brings you a continuous live view of the Duluth harbor & ship canal at:

www.duluthharborcam.com

Northern Images Photography

by Dennis O'Hara

Publisher Zenith City Press produces fine books that celebrate historic Duluth, Western Lake Superior, and Minnesota's Arrowhead and also operates Zenith City Online, a web-based publication and free public research resource updated daily. Discover more at:

www.zenithcity.com